COMPREHENSION NINJA WORKBOOK

AGES 8–9

ANDREW JENNINGS

BLOOMSBURY EDUCATION
LONDON OXFORD NEW YORK NEW DELHI SYDNEY

BLOOMSBURY EDUCATION
Bloomsbury Publishing Plc
50 Bedford Square, London, WC1B 3DP, UK
29 Earlsfort Terrace, Dublin 2, Ireland

BLOOMSBURY, BLOOMSBURY EDUCATION and the Diana logo are trademarks of
Bloomsbury Publishing Plc

First published in Great Britain, 2020 by Bloomsbury Publishing Plc
Text copyright © Andrew Jennings, 2020

Ninja illustrations copyright © Andrew Jennings, 2020
Illustrations copyright © Ilias Arahovitis, 2020

Andrew Jennings has asserted his right under the Copyright, Designs and Patents Act, 1988, to be identified as Author of this work

Bloomsbury Publishing Plc does not have any control over, or responsibility for, any third-party websites referred to or in this book. All internet addresses given in this book were correct at the time of going to press. The author and publisher regret any inconvenience caused if addresses have changed or sites have ceased to exist, but can accept no responsibility for any such changes

All rights reserved. No part of this publication may be reproduced or transmitted in any form or by any means, electronic or mechanical, including photocopying, recording, or any information storage or retrieval system, without prior permission in writing from the publishers

A catalogue record for this book is available from the British Library

ISBN: PB: 978-1-4729-8507-1; ePDF: 978-1-4729-8508-8

2 4 6 8 10 9 7 5 3

Text design by Marcus Duck Design

Printed and bound in the UK by Ashford Colour Press

This book is produced using paper that is made from wood grown in managed, sustainable forests. It is natural, renewable and recyclable. The logging and manufacturing processes conform to the environmental regulations of the country of origin.

To find out more about our authors and books visit www.bloomsbury.com and sign up for our newsletters

Acknowledgements

Without Paul Watson's supportive conversations and the inspiring words within them, Vocabulary Ninja and Comprehension Ninja would undoubtedly never have become a reality. I'm proud to call him a friend and even prouder that he could be a part of the Comprehension Ninja series.

INTRODUCTION

Reading comprehension is all about understanding what you are reading – and being able to show that you understand. This Comprehension Ninja workbook will help your child master the foundations of reading comprehension by focusing on three key aspects:

- **Skimming** and **scanning** a whole text to locate information efficiently.
- **Retrieving** the correct information from the text in eight different ways.
- **Vocabulary** awareness and the **effect of word choices.**

This book contains seven curriculum-linked texts, each followed by a set of questions to check whether your child has understood the text. There are eight question types to develop your child's comprehension skills:

 Labelling   Matching    Fill in the gap    Multiple choice

 True or false    Find and copy    Sequencing    Underline or highlight

For texts 1 - 4, the activity pages feature one question type per page so your child can focus on building up their comprehension skills one at a time, while texts 5 - 7 look a bit more like a test, with two pages of mixed questions.
This book includes the following topics: the Lake District, Anglo-Saxons, Ramadan and Eid, guide dogs, chimpanzees, Russia and Boudicca.

HOW TO USE THIS WORKBOOK

STEP 1 – READ THE TEXT CAREFULLY

Encourage your child to read the whole text carefully before they start trying to answer the questions. You can help them with any words or phrases they don't know. As an extra activity, you could ask your child to read the text aloud to you.

STEP 2 – PICK OUT KEY WORDS AND INFORMATION

Picking out key words and headings will help your child to quickly locate the information they need to answer the questions. Encourage your child to underline key information as they read the text, such as:

- **Nouns** – names of people, places and objects.
- **Time** – dates and periods of time.
- **Numbers** – amounts, statistics, percentages and figures.
- **Vocabulary** – important topic vocabulary or words they are unsure of. They could look these up online or in a dictionary to find out what they mean.

Your child should also look out for titles and headings, which will help them understand the structure of the text.

STEP 3 – IDENTIFY KEY WORDS IN THE QUESTIONS

Encourage your child to identify key words in the questions so they know what they're looking for to find the answer. For example, in a text about the seaside:

> **Question**: What might you find in a rock pool?
>
> **Key words**: rock pool

'Rock pool' is the clue needed to answer the question.

STEP 4 – SKIM AND SCAN THE TEXT

Once your child has identified the key words in the question, they can try to remember where in the text the answer can be found. This might be as simple as remembering whether it was at the beginning, middle or end of the text, or thinking about which section the key information was in.

Your child can then **skim read** the whole text to find the section they need. When they've found it, they should **scan** the section to find the relevant sentences. They then read those sentences carefully to find the answer.

Invite your child to work through all the questions and give them lots of encouragement along the way. The answers can be found at the back of the book.

1 THE LAKE DISTRICT

Have you ever visited the Lake District? This stunning part of England is breathtaking to see. It's extremely popular with tourists, having over 15 million visitors per year. It's not only a place of outstanding natural beauty, but also the home of some of England's most impressive landmarks and wonderful wildlife. It's even protected by the government, to preserve its beauty.

The Lake District – also known as the Lakes – is England's largest national park. It's located in Cumbria, in the North-West of England. There are 16 lakes in the Lake District. Most of them are called either 'meres' or 'waters'. In the Middle Ages, the word 'mere' meant pure – and, as a lake is filled with fresh water that can be drunk, this makes perfect sense. The largest lake in England can be found in the Lake District: Lake Windermere. It measures a whopping 18 km long, and it's ideal for sailing. Many visitors come to enjoy a boat ride over this fantastic lake.

Of course, the lakes see a lot of rain – it keeps them topped up! The town of Seathwaite has the highest rate of rainfall in the whole of England. It receives around 355 centimetres of rain each year.

The Lakes aren't all about water, though! The park is also mountainous, and many people visit the area to rock climb or stroll along the steep landscape. The Lake District is home to England's highest mountain: Scafell Pike. Scafell Pike stands proudly at 978 m above sea level. Just imagine getting to the top and looking down at the beautiful lakes in the valleys below – this amazing sight is why so many people take on the challenge!

* all of this items listed can be done through the Air Cadets, so there's no point doing this stuff if you can do it through the Air Cadets.

The Lakes are an ideal place for an action-packed adventure, even if you don't fancy mountain-climbing.* You could test your map-reading skills with orienteering, which is a hiking race: you use a map and compass to explore. You could go gorge walking, which involves getting very wet to scramble down into rivers and explore them. You could also try canoeing or sailing across the lakes themselves.

If you'd like a more relaxed time, you could simply sit and enjoy the view. The Lakes inspired some of the most famous English poets: William Wordsworth's poem 'I Wandered Lonely as a Cloud' was written after he saw daffodils all along the shore of one lake called Ullswater. Beatrix Potter enjoyed the scenery and wildlife of the Lakes so much that she included it in her famous Peter Rabbit stories. You could follow their examples and try watching for birds of prey such as eagles, ospreys, kites, buzzards and falcons. Back on the ground, you could keep your eyes open for rabbits, red squirrels and wild mountain ponies.

Visitors to the Lakes bring in a lot of extra money to the area – in 2017, it totalled 2.9 billion pounds! With all of this to see and do, it's no wonder that there were over 15 million of them! Why not become one yourself?

1 THE LAKE DISTRICT

FILL IN THE GAP

Read the sentences and choose the correct word to fill the gap. Look back at paragraphs one and two in *The Lake District* to find the correct answer.

This stunning part of _____england_____ is breathtaking to see.

There are 16 _____lakes_____ in the Lake District.

It's extremely popular with tourists, having over 15 million _____vistiors_____ per year.

It's even _____protected_____ by the government, to preserve its beauty.

The largest lake in England can be found in the Lake District: Lake _____windermere_____.

Look back at paragraphs three and four in *The Lake District* to find the correct answer.

The park is also mountainous, and many people visit the area to rock climb or stroll along the _____steep_____ landscape.

The town of Seathwaite has the highest rate of _____rain_____ in the whole of England.

Scafell Pike stands _____proudly_____ at 978 m above sea level.

Look back at *The Lake District* to find the correct answer.

The Lakes is an ideal place for an action-packed _____adventure_____, even if you don't fancy mountain-climbing.

Beatrix Potter enjoyed the scenery and wildlife of the Lakes so much that she included it in her _____famous_____ Peter Rabbit stories.

You could also try _____canoeing_____ or sailing across the lakes themselves.

Visitors to the Lakes bring in a lot of extra money to the area - in 2017, it totalled 2.9 _____billion_____ pounds!

1 THE LAKE DISTRICT

MATCHING

Draw a line with a ruler to match the information.

Lake District	largest lake in England
Lake Windermere	England's highest mountain
Scafell Pike	the Lakes
Seathwaite	highest rate of rainfall

Draw a line with a ruler to match the information.

visitors per year	978 m
above sea level	18 km
largest lake	355 cm per year
rate of rainfall	over 15 million

Draw a line with a ruler to match the information.

William Wordsworth	Peter Rabbit
Beatrix Potter	I Wandered Lonely as a Cloud
orienteering	scramble down into rivers
gorge walking	hiking race

7

1 THE LAKE DISTRICT

◉ MULTIPLE CHOICE

Circle the correct answer to the following questions.

How many people visit the Lake District every year?

| over 13 million | 14 million | over 15 million | 16 million |

What did the word 'mere' mean in the Middle Ages?

| fresh | pure | water | clear |

Why do people take on the challenge of Scafell Pike?

| to enjoy the amazing sight | to go orienteering | to go gorge walking | to try mountain-climbing |

How long is Lake Windermere?

| 18 mm | 18 cm | 18 m | 18 km |

Who was inspired by the views of the Lakes?

| Harry Potter | Peter Rabbit | William Shakespeare | Beatrix Potter |

Which town has the highest rate of rainfall in the whole of England?

| Windermere | Seathwaite | Cumbria | Ullswater |

Which animals might you see if you visit the Lakes?

| horses | grey squirrels | red squirrels | hares |

Which year did visitors to the Lakes bring in 2.9 billion pounds to the area?

| 2015 | 2016 | 2017 | 2018 |

1 THE LAKE DISTRICT

👎 TRUE OR FALSE

Read the sentences. Put a tick in the correct box to show which sentences are *true* and which are *false*.

Statement	True	False
The Lake District has over 14 million visitors per year.		✓
The Lake District is in north-east England.	✓	
There are 17 lakes in the Lake District.		✓
'Mere' meant pure.	✓	
The largest lake is called Ullswater.		✓
The Lake District is protected by the Lake District Police.		
Seathwaite has the highest rate of rainfall in the whole of England.		✓
Scafell Pike is over 1000 m above sea level.		✓
Wild mountain ponies can be found in the Lake District.		✓
The Lake District is England's second largest national park.		✓
Beatrix Potter included the Lakes in the Peter Rabbit stories.	✓	
Lake Windermere is the smallest lake in England.		✓
2.9 billion pounds were brought in by visitors in 2017.	✓	
People enjoy boat rides over Lake Windermere.		✓
You can go gorge walking in the Lakes.	✓	

2 ANGLO-SAXONS

For thousands of years, Great Britain's history was a stream of invasions and settlers. Between about 200 BCE and 43 CE, this small island was partially populated by warriors from Gaul (the part of Europe that is now France and Belgium), who had a big influence on the language. Then the Romans took over, bringing countless customs with them. Over time, these people all became Britons – but before that, there were some epic struggles for power!

Replacing Romans

After the end of Roman rule in Britain, in around 410 CE, new invaders arrived. Tribes from Europe combined to take over Britain. The largest and most powerful were the Angles, the Saxons and the Jutes. Each tribe came from a different part of Europe. The Angles were from what is now southern Denmark, the Jutes were northern Danes, and the Saxons hailed from Germany and the Netherlands. These tribes crossed the North Sea and ruled Britain until 1066. We now call these invaders 'Anglo-Saxons'.

Anglo-Saxon life

In an Anglo-Saxon village, you would be considered an adult at the age of ten. You'd have far bigger worries than homework from school! You'd have to work as hard as adults three or four times your age. If you did anything wrong, you would also be punished as an adult.

Girls would join the women who tended to the home by cooking meals, weaving cloth and brewing ale. Boys would be trained in the same trades as their fathers: if your father made spears, so did you; if he ploughed fields, you did that.

The Anglo-Saxons brought new languages that replaced much of the Latin the Romans had used. They merged together and formed a language now known as 'old English' – which, unsurprisingly, eventually became English as we know it! Despite this, very few Anglo-Saxons in Britain could read.

More invaders!

Vikings, from what we now call Denmark and Norway, invaded Britain between around 787 and 1066. They also made an impact on language: many of the words used only in the Midlands and the north of England are Viking terms.

The Vikings and Anglo-Saxons divided up the country. Over the next 200 years, some kings of England were Viking, and some were Anglo-Saxon. In 1066, the Anglo-Saxon King Edward died, and Harold Godwinson was crowned in his place.

However, others felt they had a claim to the throne – leading to even more people invading! First to arrive was an army from Norway, led by Harald Hardrada – but he was defeated. Immediately afterwards, though, when the Anglo-Saxon army was exhausted, the Normans invaded from France.

The great era of the Anglo-Saxons was over, and England was ruled by the Normans.

The Anglo-Saxons still have a lasting impact on a lot that we do, though. In fact, the name they gave to the part of Britain they ruled was 'Angle-land' – which, through time, became 'England'!

2 ANGLO-SAXONS

FILL IN THE GAP

Read the sentences and choose the correct word to fill the gap. Look back at *Anglo-Saxons* to find the correct answer.

For thousands of years, Great Britain's history was a stream of ___invader___ and settlers.

Then the Romans took over, bringing countless ___cousterms___ with them.

In an Anglo-Saxon ___villiage___, you would be considered an adult at the age of ten.

Each ___tribe___ came from a different part of Europe.

In 1066, the Anglo-Saxon ___king___ Edward died, and Harold Godwinson was crowned in his place.

The largest and most ___powerful___ were the Angles, the Saxons and the Jutes.

In fact, the name they gave to the part of Britain they ruled was 'Angle-land' – which, through time, became '___england___'!

The Anglo-Saxons brought new ___words___ that replaced much of the Latin the Romans had used.

Girls would join the women who ___stayed___ to the home by cooking meals, weaving cloth and brewing ale.

If you did anything wrong, you would also be ___punished___ as an adult.

Despite this, very few Anglo-Saxons in Britain could ___read___.

These tribes ___ruled___ the North Sea and ruled Britain until 1066.

2 ANGLO-SAXONS
MATCHING

Draw a line with a ruler to match the information.

new invaders arrived	787 to 1066
Vikings invaded Britain	200 BCE to 43 CE
partially populated by warriors from Gaul	410 CE
King Edward died	1066

Draw a line with a ruler to match the information.

Angles	northern Danes
Saxons	Denmark and Norway
Vikings	Germany and the Netherlands
Jutes	southern Denmark

Draw a line with a ruler to match the information.

girls	cooking meals
boys	England
adult	same trade as fathers
Angle-land	age of ten

2 ANGLO-SAXONS

◉ MULTIPLE CHOICE

Circle the correct answer to the following questions.

Where did the tribes who combined to take over Britain come from?

| Africa | Asia | Europe | America |

What did the Romans bring with them when they took over?

| water | customs | clothes | animals |

What was the name of the Anglo-Saxon king?

| Edward | Harold | Harald | Edwin |

What age were Anglo-Saxons considered to be adults?

| eight | nine | ten | eleven |

Which sea did the tribes cross to come to England?

| Norwegian Sea | Yellow Sea | Scotia Sea | North Sea |

What was the name of the leader of the invasion from Norway?

| Harold Godwinson | Harold Hardrada | Harald Hardrada | Harald Godwinson |

Which year did King Edward die?

| 1056 | 1065 | 1066 | 1075 |

Where do many words used only in the Midlands and North of England come from?

| the Vikings | the Angles | the Jutes | the Saxons |

2 ANGLO-SAXONS
TRUE OR FALSE

Read the sentences. Put a tick in the correct box to show which sentences are *true* and which are *false*.

Statement	True	False
New invaders arrived in around 410 CE.	✓	
England was originally known as Angle-land.	✓	
Harald Hardrada led the Anglo-Saxon army.		✓
The Angles were from what is now southern France.		✓
The Anglo-Saxon king was called Edward.	✓	✓
Harold Godwinson was crowned king.	✓	✓
The Normans ruled England after the Anglo-Saxons.		✓
The Anglo-Saxons brought new languages.	✓	
Romans used Latin as their language.		
All Anglo-Saxons in Britain could read.		✓
The first army to arrive from Norway was led by Harold Godwinson.		✓
The Romans brought countless customs with them.	✓	
Anglo-Saxon boys were trained in the same trades as their fathers.	✓	
The Saxons came from southern Denmark.		
King Edward died in 1055.		

2 ANGLO-SAXONS
FIND AND COPY

These questions are about *Anglo-Saxons*.

Look at paragraph one. Find and copy a word that suggests that over time people made Britain their permanent home.

_____impact_____

Look at the paragraph beginning 'After the end of Roman rule…'. Find and copy the word that suggests that tribes from Europe came to invade Britain.

_____invaders_____

Look at the paragraph beginning 'Girls would join the women…'. Find and copy a word that suggests that girls and women were responsible for and looked after the home.

_____

Look at the paragraph beginning 'Vikings, from what we…'. Find and copy a word that suggests that the Vikings influenced language.

_____impact_____

2 ANGLO-SAXONS

UNDERLINE OR HIGHLIGHT

Read the paragraphs below and then follow the instructions.

> The Vikings and Anglo-Saxons divided up the country. Over the next 200 years, some kings of England were Viking, and some were Anglo-Saxon. In 1066, the Anglo-Saxon King Edward died, and Harold Godwinson was crowned in his place.
>
> However, others felt they had a claim to the throne – leading to even more people invading! First to arrive was an army from Norway, led by Harald Hardrada – but he was defeated. Immediately afterwards, though, when the Anglo-Saxon army was exhausted, the Normans invaded from France.

Underline or highlight a word that means to separate into parts.

Underline or highlight a word that means a male ruler.

Underline or highlight a word that means an organised military force.

Underline or highlight a word that means instantly.

Underline or highlight a word that tells us that the Anglo-Saxon army was very tired.

3 RAMADAN AND EID

Islam is the world's second-largest religion. It has over 1.8 billion followers, who are known as Muslims – that's 24% of the world's population. 50 countries have mainly Muslim populations.

Muslims, like people of many other religions, celebrate rituals and holidays that are a key part of their yearly calendar. Muslims all over the world take part in the traditions of Ramadan and Eid al-Fitr. These events go hand in hand as one: Eid comes at the end of Ramadan.

Ramadan is the ninth month in the Islamic calendar. This calendar is different from the one most people in Europe use: it is a 'lunar' calendar, which means that the dates relate to the cycles of the moon. The dates of lunar months change from year to year. This includes Ramadan, so the date when Eid is celebrated also changes.

During the month of Ramadan, Muslims vow to fast, which means they commit not to eat or drink. They believe that the difficulty of fasting helps them to turn their attention inwards and focus on their faith.

Each day, for the whole month, Muslims fast between dawn and sunset. Depending on the time of year Ramadan falls, and the location in the world where it is practised, daylight hours will vary. For example, when Ramadan falls in December for Muslims in the UK, the days are short so fasting may last only eight hours. If it falls in June, daylight could last more than 16 hours. This means that some Muslims will face a sterner test of their faith than others.

Some people are not required to fast in Islamic law, to ensure that everybody can stay fit and healthy. They include people who are very young or very old, pregnant, breastfeeding, ill, menstruating or travelling long distances. However, many people who could fall into these categories choose to fast anyway.

Fasting during Ramadan is an extremely important way for Muslims to show their devotion to their faith. It is one of the Five Pillars of Islam, along with faith, charity, prayer and a journey to the holy city of Mecca. The journey should happen at least once in a Muslim's lifetime. Faith, charity and prayer should be displayed in a Muslim's life every day. They are a part of Ramadan, too: Muslims pray and show their faith when fasting, and their support of each other is a way of showing charity.

At the end of Ramadan is Eid, which is traditionally celebrated for up to three days. Eid is a huge celebration: Muslims celebrate the end of Ramadan and the breaking of their fasts by coming together to pray and hold feasts. Mosques and the local community prepare a vast range of foods to enjoy. Sweet foods are particularly popular.

Even if you have not taken part in the fasting, you can take part in the celebration. In fact, it is not permitted to fast during Eid!

3 RAMADAN AND EID

✏️ FILL IN THE GAP

Read the sentences and choose the correct word to fill the gap. Look back at *Ramadan and Eid* to find the correct answer.

Islam is the world's second-largest ____religon____.

Each day, for the whole month, Muslims fast between ____Sunrise____ and sunset.

These events go hand in hand as one: Eid comes at the ____start____ of Ramadan.

During the month of Ramadan, Muslims vow to fast, which means they commit not to ____eat____ or drink.

____mulisms____ and the local community prepare a vast range of foods to enjoy.

The ____fast____ should happen at least once in a Muslim's lifetime.

____fasting____ during Ramadan is an extremely important way for Muslims to show their devotion to their faith.

They are a part of Ramadan, too: Muslims pray and show their faith when fasting, and their support of each other is a way of showing ____devotion____.

Ramadan is the ____ninth____ month in the Islamic calendar.

The dates of ____Islamic____ months change from year to year.

They believe that the ____difficuly____ of fasting helps them to turn their attention inwards and focus on their faith.

Faith, charity and ____player____ should be displayed in a Muslim's life every day.

3 RAMADAN AND EID

MATCHING

Draw a line with a ruler to match the information.

Muslim	follower of Islam
Islam	huge celebration
Eid	ninth month
Ramadan	second-largest religion

Draw a line with a ruler to match the information.

Islamic calendar	focus on their faith
difficulty of fasting helps	lunar calendar
not required to fast	devotion to faith
fasting shows	very young or very old

Draw a line with a ruler to match the information.

Mecca	popular
fasting	holy city
sweet foods	cycles of the moon
lunar calendar	between dawn and sunset

3 RAMADAN AND EID
LABEL

Label the information with the correct word or words.

Holy city	mecca
Celebration that comes at the end of Ramadan	Eid
Fasting, faith, charity, prayer and pilgrimage	every day life
A follower of Islam	musliem
World's second-largest religion	Islam
Length of Ramadan	~~4~~ 30 days

Label the information with the correct word or words.

Popular foods during Eid	sweets
Celebration when it's not permitted to fast	Eid
Length of Eid	3 days
The month in the Islamic calendar that Ramadan takes place	ninth
1.8 billion followers	Islam
Length of fast each day	sun rise to sunset

Draw the statement in the boxes. Add your own labels to your drawing.

a calendar	people eating a meal
people cooking food	Muslims coming together to pray

3 RAMADAN AND EID
123 SEQUENCING

Look at the sentences below. Write the numbers 1 to 4 to show the order the words occur in the sentences.

Mosques and the local community prepare a vast range of foods to enjoy. Sweet foods are particularly popular.

3	2	1	4
enjoy	range	community	popular

Look at *Ramadan and Eid*. Number the statements from 1 to 5 to show the order they occur in the text.

50 countries have mainly Muslim populations. — 1

Muslims all over the world take part in the traditions of Ramadan and Eid. — 2

It is one of the Five Pillars of Islam, along with faith, charity, prayer and a journey to the holy city of Mecca. — 3

Each day, for the whole month, Muslims fast between dawn and sunset. — 4

Even if you have not taken part in the fasting, you can take part in the celebration. — 5

Look at *Ramadan and Eid*. Number the statements from 1 to 5 to show the order they occur in the text. Look at the first line of each paragraph to help you.

Eid is a huge celebration: Muslims celebrate the end of Ramadan and the breaking of their fasts by coming together to pray and hold feasts. — 4

These events go hand in hand as one: Eid comes at the end of Ramadan. — 5

They include people who are very young or very old, pregnant, breastfeeding, ill, menstruating or travelling long distances. — 3

Faith, charity and prayer should be displayed in a Muslim's life every day. — 2

Depending on the time of year Ramadan falls, and the location in the world where it is practised, daylight hours will vary. — 1

3 RAMADAN AND EID

FIND AND COPY

These questions are about *Ramadan and Eid*.

Look at paragraph one. Find and copy a word that suggests all of the inhabitants of the world.

_____Population_____

Look at the paragraph beginning 'During the month of Ramadan….'. Find and copy a word that suggests that Muslims make a promise to fast.

_____breaking_____

Look at the paragraph beginning 'At the end of Ramadan is….'. Find and copy a word that suggests sweet foods are particularly liked.

_____Popular_____

Look at the paragraph beginning 'At the end of Ramadan is….'. Find and copy a word that suggests a social gathering or enjoyable activity held to acknowledge a happy day.

_____Commuity_____

3 RAMADAN AND EID
UNDERLINE OR HIGHLIGHT

Read the paragraphs below and then follow the instructions.

> During the month of Ramadan, Muslims vow to fast, which means they commit not to eat or drink. They believe that the difficulty of fasting helps them to turn their attention inwards and focus on their faith.
>
> Each day, for the whole month, Muslims fast between dawn and sunset. Depending on the time of year Ramadan falls, and the location in the world where it is practised, daylight hours will vary. For example, when Ramadan falls in December for Muslims in the UK, the days are short so fasting may last only eight hours. If it falls in June, daylight could last more than 16 hours. This means that some Muslims will face a sterner test of their faith than others.

Underline or highlight a word that means to not eat or drink.

Underline or highlight a word that means something is not easy to do.

Underline or highlight a word that means the time in the evening when the sun disappears.

Underline or highlight a word that means to differ or change.

Underline or highlight a word that means a strong belief in a religion.

4 GUIDE DOGS

Humans have had a special relationship with dogs for thousands of years. Dogs have been kept for hunting and protection – although nowadays they're more often chosen for companionship and fun! Some relationships between pets and their owners are truly remarkable. For some people, their dogs are the only things that allow them to interact with the world around them.

Guide dogs are trained to assist blind or partially-sighted people. They look out for obstacles in their owners' paths. Many are also trained to fetch help or find doorways.

Guide dogs for the blind are mentioned in writing as long ago as the 1500s, but the first modern training was done after World War II. The idea was born in Germany and Switzerland. There, assistance dogs were used to help war veterans who had been blinded. In 1927, an American dog breeder called Dorothy Eustis wrote about them and took the idea to the USA. She started 'The Seeing Eye', her first guide dog school.

Schools in the United Kingdom soon followed, due to the work of Muriel Crooke and Rosamund Bond. They had heard about 'The Seeing Eye' and contacted Dorothy Eustis. Dorothy sent one of her trainers to the United Kingdom in 1930. Within a year, Muriel and Rosamund had fully trained four guide dogs. Three years later, the British Guide Dog Association was founded – and it still helps people to find guide dogs today.

Training a guide dog

Training a guide dog takes many years and a lot of work. There are seven stages to a guide dog's life.

1. A guide dog puppy, usually a Golden Retriever, Labrador or German Shepherd, is born into the home of a dedicated volunteer. It will stay here for the first six weeks of its life.

2. The puppy takes its first test, which assesses its character. This is a good indicator for whether it's suitable to be a guide dog.

3. The puppy spends a year with puppy trainers, who teach it to be obedient and follow basic commands like 'sit', 'stay' and 'come'. The puppy has to prove that it isn't easily distracted!

4. When it's 14 months old, the young dog goes to one of four national centres for the first stage of its training. It learns to follow precise commands.

5. The guide dog then moves to a local training centre for the secondary stage of its learning. This is when things become more difficult: the dog has to learn to sense, recognise and avoid risks.

6. Having mastered its training, the successful dog graduates.

7. The dog and an owner are paired up. The bond between them has to be close and natural, so finding a good match can take a while. When they finally meet, the dog and its owner will rely on each other for years.

Owning a dog can be very expensive – and training guide dogs costs even more. On average, the cost to train a guide dog is around £44,600. What price would you put on being able to see?

Label the information with the correct stage of training.

graduation	The Dog Graducation
born with dedicated volunteer	
national training centre	
spend a year with puppy trainers	
local training centre	
suitability checks	

Label the description with the correct information.

common breed of guide dogs	
year a dog trainer arrived in UK	1930
American dog trainer	
British dog trainers	
humans that dogs help	blind People
age guide dogs go to national training centre	

Draw the statement in the boxes. Add your own labels to your drawing.

(drawing of a dog)	
the first year with a trainer	graduation
reasons to keep dogs	dogs and owners meeting

4 GUIDE DOGS
123 SEQUENCING

Look at the sentences below. Write the numbers 1 to 4 to show the order the words occur in the sentences.

The guide dog then moves to a local training centre for the secondary stage of its learning. This is when things become more difficult: the dog has to learn to sense, recognise and avoid risks.

secondary	recognise	local	stage

Look at the 'Training a guide dog' section in *Guide dogs*. Number the statements from 1 to 5 to show the order they occur in the text.

The puppy spends a year with puppy trainers, who teach it to be obedient and follow basic commands like 'sit', 'stay' and 'come'. ☐ 2

There are seven stages to a guide dog's life. ☐ 3

It will stay here for the first six weeks of its life. ☐ 1

The puppy has to prove that it isn't easily distracted! ☐ 5

The puppy takes its first test, which assesses its character. ☐ 4

Look at *Guide dogs*. Number the statements from 1 to 5 to show the order they occur in the text. Look at the first line of each paragraph to help you.

Humans have had a special relationship with dogs for thousands of years. ☐ 1

Guide dogs for the blind are mentioned in writing as long ago as the 1500s, but the first modern training was done after World War II. ☐ 2

Owning a dog can be very expensive – and training guide dogs costs even more. ☐ 5

Guide dogs are trained to assist blind or partially-sighted people. ☐ 3

Schools in the United Kingdom soon followed, due to the work of Muriel Crooke and Rosamund Bond. ☐ 4

4 GUIDE DOGS
⊙ MULTIPLE CHOICE

Circle the correct answer to the following questions.

When did people start training guide dogs in the UK?

| 1920 ✓ | 1930 | 1940 | 1950 |

How many guide dogs were trained in the first year in the UK?

| one | two | three | four |

How many stages are there to a guide dog's training?

| four | five | six | seven |

What is the final stage of a guide dog's training?

| national training centre | being matched to an owner | retirement | local training centre |

Which dog breed is not commonly used as a guide dog?

| Labrador | German Shepherd | St Bernard | Golden Retriever |

It is important that guide dogs do not become…

| too old | lazy | overweight | distracted |

How old is a guide dog puppy when it goes to a national training centre?

| four months | 14 months | 20 months | 24 months |

What is the average cost to train a guide dog?

| £44,600 | £44,660 | £46,600 | £64,600 |

30

4 GUIDE DOGS
👎 TRUE OR FALSE

Read the sentences. Put a tick in the correct box to show which sentences are *true* and which are *false*.

Statement	True	False
Training guide dogs in the UK started in the 1940s.		✓
The British Guide Dog Association was founded to help people to find guide dogs.	✓	
There are six stages to a guide dog's training.		✓
The final stage in a guide dog's training is finding an owner.	✓	
People have kept dogs for protection.	✓	
Labradors are the only dog breed that can be trained as a guide dog.		✓
There are 14 national training centres for guide dogs.	✓	
When a dog graduates it is then matched with an owner.	✓	
Dorothy Eustis created The Seeing Eye in America.	✓	
Dogs are sometimes kept and used for hunting.		✓
After training at a local centre, guide dogs then move to a national training centre.	✓	
On average, it costs over £50,000 to train a guide dog.		✓
Four guide dogs were trained in the UK in 1930.		✓
People keep dogs for companionship.	✓	
Guide dogs help humans interact with the world around them.	✓	

4 GUIDE DOGS
FIND AND COPY

These questions are about *Guide dogs*.

Look at paragraph one. Find and copy a word that suggests people kept dogs for a sense of friendship.

companionship
~~compassion~~

Look at paragraph one. Find and copy a word that suggests people kept dogs to help them stay safe.

interat

Look at paragraph one. Find and copy a word that suggests people can communicate or be involved with their environment.

_____

Look at the second paragraph. Find and copy a word that suggests some humans might have some sight.

partially

4 GUIDE DOGS
UNDERLINE OR HIGHLIGHT

Read the paragraphs below and then follow the instructions.

> Training a guide dog takes <u>many years</u> and a lot of work. There are seven stages to a guide dog's life.
>
> 1. A guide dog puppy, usually a Golden Retriever, Labrador or German Shepherd, is born into the home of a dedicated volunteer. It will stay here for the first six weeks of its life.
>
> 2. The puppy takes its first test, which assesses its character. This is a good indicator for whether it's <u>suitable</u> to be a guide dog.
>
> 3. The puppy spends a year with puppy trainers, who teach it to be obedient and follow basic <u>commands</u> like 'sit', 'stay' and 'come'. The puppy has to prove that it isn't easily <u>distracted</u>!

Underline or highlight a word that means to be devoted to a task or role.

Underline or highlight a word that means a process that checks suitability.

Underline or highlight a word that means to be a good fit for a role.

Underline or highlight a word that means to comply with orders given.

Underline or highlight a word that means to lose focus on the task you are doing.

5 CHIMPANZEES

What are chimpanzees?

Chimpanzees are beautiful, intelligent animals that have a lot in common with humans. Although they look similar to monkeys, chimpanzees are actually part of the ape family, and are related to gorillas and orangutans.

Are they endangered?

Chimpanzees are endangered. They're at risk partly because of their habitat being cut down and partly because they are hunted for meat or to be sold into captivity. Over the last 100 years, the number of chimpanzees living in the wild has dropped by over 700,000.

What is the chimpanzees' habitat?

In the wild, chimpanzees are found on the continent of Africa, in roughly 20 different countries. They are adaptable creatures and can thrive in diverse habitats from humid forests to dry savannahs. They build shelters and comfortable beds from leaves.

What do they eat?

Like humans, chimpanzees are omnivores: they eat a wide variety of foods, including both meat and plants. They enjoy eating fruit, nuts, insects, lizards, frogs and even small monkeys.

What is a chimpanzee's life like?

Chimpanzees are social animals that live in groups. They have strong family bonds: a mother carries her baby on her back for the first four years of its life. Offspring and parents remain extremely close, although young females usually leave their parents at adolescence to start their own families. A male chimpanzee remains with his mother's family for his lifetime, which is approximately 45 years in the wild.

Groups of chimpanzees have complicated power structures. Males fight for dominance, but they also form close friendships. Often, friendships help the males to protect themselves or fight for dominance as a group. Males also work together to hunt and to protect their groups.

Females and males work together to bring up their babies, to share skills and food, and to maintain the group's health through cleanliness: they comb and clean each other's hair.

What can chimpanzees do?

Chimpanzees are some of the most intelligent animals on the Earth. They communicate with each other by panting, drumming or using gestures and facial expressions. Their communication skills, like those of humans, allow them to learn. They use sticks and rocks as simple tools, for example to find small animals and to open nuts. They use chewed leaves to make sponges to help them drink water.

Chimpanzees' intelligence even allows them to communicate with humans. In conservation, many have been taught to use flashcards and sign language. By 'talking' to chimpanzees like this, scientists have discovered that they have excellent memories, and they feel complex emotions like grief and regret.

Chimpanzees' abilities also mean they are used for tests considered too risky for humans. The first American in space was actually a chimpanzee called Ham. In 1961, he was taught by astronauts to perform simple commands to test reactions in space. His space suit was also tested, during a period of lost pressure. Ham survived and the mission was considered a success. Under ten years later, in 1969, the first human Americans stepped onto the moon.

FILL IN THE GAP

Look back at *Chimpanzees*. Skim to find the correct area or paragraph of the text. Then scan to locate the correct sentence. Fill in the gap with the missing word.

Females and males work together to bring up their babies, to share skills and food, and to maintain the group's health through cleanliness: they _____comb_____ and clean each other's hair.

A male chimpanzee remains with his mother's family for his lifetime, which is approximately _____45_____ years in the wild.

MATCHING

Draw a line with a ruler to match the information.

chimpanzee who went into space	rocks
used by chimpanzees to open nuts	complex emotions
chimpanzees feel	Ham

LABEL

Label the description with the correct year or number.

number of chimpanzees living in the wild has dropped by	700,00
year human Americans went into space	1969
year Ham went into space	1981
years chimpanzees live for	45 years
number of countries that wild chimpanzees are found in	20 countries

TRUE OR FALSE

Read the sentences. Put a tick in the correct box to show which sentences are *true* and which are *false*.

Ham the chimpanzee went into space. True ☐ False ☐

Chimpanzees use tools to catch food. True ☐ False ☑

Male chimpanzees often leave their parents at adolescence to start their own families. True ☐ False ☑

◎ MULTIPLE CHOICE

Circle the correct answer to the following question.

How long do mother chimpanzees carry their babies on their backs?

| two years | three years | four years ✓ | five years |

123 SEQUENCING

Look at *Chimpanzees*. Number the statements from 1 to 3 to show the order they occur in the text.

The first American in space was actually a chimpanzee called Ham.	1
Chimpanzees' intelligence even allows them to communicate with humans.	3
Under ten years later, in 1969, the first human Americans stepped onto the moon.	2

👀 FIND AND COPY

Read the sentence below. Find and copy a word that suggests that humans showed Ham how to control the spacecraft.

In 1961, he was taught by astronauts to perform simple commands to test reactions in space.

command

✋ UNDERLINE OR HIGHLIGHT

Read the sentences below. Underline or highlight a word that means physically relaxed.

> They are <u>adaptable</u> creatures and can thrive in diverse habitats from humid forests to dry savannahs. They build shelters and comfortable beds from leaves.

6 COUNTRY STUDY: RUSSIA

Although countries can be impressive in lots of ways, Russia is the most impressive in terms of size. It is geographically the largest country in the world. It covers one tenth of all the land on Earth and stretches across 11 different time zones! It has only the ninth-largest population, though, at just under 147 million people.

The capital city of Russia is Moscow. It has a population of 12.2 million and is the largest city in Europe. It is famous for its architecture, which includes the two tallest buildings in Europe and the stunning, historic St Basil's Cathedral. St Petersburg is Russia's second-largest city, with five million inhabitants. It also boasts some breathtakingly beautiful buildings and a famous statue called The Bronze Horseman.

Russia has lots of neighbours. Although it is part of Europe, it also borders a number of Asian countries. In Europe, to its west, it is met by Azerbaijan, Belarus, Estonia, Finland and Poland, among others. To its south, Asian countries including China, Mongolia and Kazakhstan border it.

Russia also has shores on three different oceans: the warm Pacific, the Atlantic and the freezing Arctic. As a consequence, it is home to shipping ports for military, fishing and pleasure ships and is considered to be a maritime giant across the world. Its major rivers include the Amur, Irtysh, Altay, Lena, Ob, Yenisey and Volga. The Volga is the longest river in Russia, at 3,700 kilometres.

*and for attacking ukraine

Russia's traditional foods, naturally, use a lot of fish. Russia is also famous for caviar – which is fish eggs. Caviar can be extraordinarily expensive. The Russian variety called Almas has the highest cost in the world: per gram, it costs almost as much as diamonds. How much would you pay to eat fish eggs?

Unsurprisingly, given its size, Russia has landscapes both by the water and inland that differ extremely. They include habitats from cold, almost arctic plains called 'tundra', through leafy forests, to hot, sandy deserts. It also has beaches with a climate similar to Spain's. Its warmest city is Sochi, by the Black Sea. Its coldest is Yatutsk, only 450 kilometres south of the Arctic Circle. This is the coldest city in the world.

Russia also boasts mountain ranges, including the Altai, Ural and Crimean Mountains. These snowy peaks are very popular for skiing with both locals and tourists. Tourist skiing holidays in the Russian mountains bring money and employment to the people in some of Russia's most hostile climates.

This diversity means there is also a lot of variety in Russia's wildlife. The snowy wastes and Arctic Ocean are home to reindeer, arctic foxes, seals and walruses. There are bears, wolves and lynxes in the forests, as well as elk, which are deer of up to 3 metres in height. In the mountains, you could find wild goats and sheep, antelopes – and more bears! Russia is also home to the Siberian tiger and Amur leopard, which are extremely endangered.

You could be as picky as you liked: with the variety of its cities, wilderness, weather and activities, there's sure to be something in Russia you would enjoy!

COUNTRY STUDY: RUSSIA

FILL IN THE GAP

Look back at *Country study: Russia*. Skim to find the correct area or paragraph of the text. Then scan to locate the correct sentence. Fill in the gap with the missing word.

Russia also has shores on three different ____oceans____: the warm Pacific, the Atlantic and the freezing Arctic.

They include habitats from cold, almost arctic plains called _____, through leafy forests, to hot, sandy deserts.

MATCHING

Draw a line with a ruler to match the information.

fish eggs	Moscow
mountain range	caviar
capital city	Altai

(fish eggs → caviar; mountain range → Altai; capital city → Moscow)

LABEL

Label the description with the correct number or place.

Russia's population	147 million
number of different time zones	4
length of Russia's longest river	3,200 kilometres
Moscow population	12.2 million
coldest city in the world	Yutatsk

TRUE OR FALSE

Read the sentences. Put a tick in the correct box to show which sentences are *true* and which are *false*.

People visit Russia to ski.	True ✓	False ☐
Australia borders Russia.	True ☐	False ☐
Russia is the second-largest country in the world.	True ☐	False ✓

⊚ MULTIPLE CHOICE

Circle the correct answer to the following question.

Which seafood is Russia famous for?

| fish | lobster | crab | (caviar) |

123 SEQUENCING

Look at *Country study: Russia*. Number the statements from 1 to 3 to show the order they occur in the text.

These snowy peaks are very popular for skiing with both locals and tourists.	2
Russia also boasts mountain ranges, including the Altai, Ural and Crimean Mountains.	1
Tourist skiing holidays in the Russian mountains bring money and employment to the people in some of Russia's most hostile climates.	3

👀 FIND AND COPY

Read the sentence below. Find and copy a word that suggests that the buildings are so amazing that they take your breath away.

It also boasts some breathtakingly beautiful buildings and a famous statue called The Bronze Horseman.

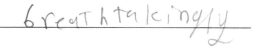

breathtakingly

✎ UNDERLINE OR HIGHLIGHT

Read the sentence below. Underline or highlight a word that means connected to the sea and linked to trade.

As a consequence, it is home to <u>shipping ports</u> for military, fishing and pleasure ships and is considered to be a maritime giant across the world.

7 BOUDICCA

Fierce women are found throughout history. They don't come much fiercer than Boudicca, Queen of the Iceni people. Her fight against the Romans over a broken promise meant she was remembered centuries after her death.

Boudicca's beginnings

Boudicca was a privileged woman. She was the wife of Prasutagus, an independent ally of Rome who was allowed to rule over the Iceni kingdom while the Romans ruled much of Britain. For years, she lived alongside the Romans peacefully.

Death and disaster

The Romans' peaceful truce with the Iceni, though, lasted only until Prasutagus's death. His will stated that his daughters should rule his kingdom alongside the Romans – but the Romans dismissed it. Only men could inherit land by Roman law, so they seized control of the whole kingdom. Boudicca was whipped, her daughters were assaulted, and the wealth and lands of the Iceni were confiscated.

The fate of the Iceni could have been decided then but, thanks to Boudicca, the Romans' betrayal was instead the start of a war.

The warrior queen

Boudicca was a clever leader and proved it with her strategies of attack. She chose to exploit the period when the Roman governor Suetonius led his troops to attack Anglesey. The Iceni and their allies the Trinovantes, led by Boudicca, marched to Camulodunum (now known as Colchester). There were few soldiers left in the city, and after two days it was entirely destroyed.

Boudicca's warriors then marched on to the new settlement of Londinium (now London, the largest city in Britain). In Londoninium, they took no prisoners. They burned the settlement to the ground, killing everyone they met. Suetonius saw the vicious attack and did not fight it. He and his troops let Londinium burn.

The Battle of Watling Street

Next, the Iceni marched to Verulamium (now St Albans). They defeated any Romans in their path – but Suetonius used the time to gather and prepare his army. When Boudicca prepared to face the Romans, it was with an army that had grown to around 300,000 angry Britons. It seemed that the Romans didn't stand a chance: they were vastly outnumbered. Suetonius positioned his men cleverly, though, and the Romans were far more sophisticated soldiers. At the Battle of Watling Street, using their superior weapons, armour and knowledge in battle, they used a V-formation to face wave after wave of British warriors – and won.

The end of the road

The Romans now understood Boudicca's power and determination. They had let her live after their betrayal, but would not make that mistake again – and Boudicca knew it. Historians of the time tell us that, refusing to let herself be taken as a prisoner, Boudicca took a final stand: she poisoned herself to prevent capture.

Although she lived almost 2,000 years ago, Boudicca will never be forgotten. A statue in remembrance of her was erected in Westminster, London, in 1902. This warrior woman, who stood up to the might of the Roman army, is the perfect example of someone who never gave up and never surrendered.

7 BOUDICCA

FILL IN THE GAP

Look back at *Boudicca*. Skim to find the correct area or paragraph of the text. Then scan to locate the correct sentence. Fill in the gap with the missing word.

Fierce women are found throughout history. They don't come much fiercer than Boudicca, _queen_ of the Iceni people.

She was the wife of _Prasutagus_, an independent ally of _Rome_ who was allowed to rule over the Iceni kingdom while the Romans ruled much of Britain.

MATCHING

Draw a line with a ruler to match the information.

Londinium	Colchester
Camulodunum	St Albans
Verulamium	London

(Londinium → London; Camulodunum → Colchester; Verulamium → St Albans)

LABEL

Label the description with person, place or date.

Queen of Iceni people	Boudicca, England 2001
King of the Iceni people	Prasutagus
place attacked by Suetonius	Anglesey
poisoned herself to prevent capture	Boudicca
year statue of Boudicca erected in London	1902

TRUE OR FALSE

Read the sentences. Put a tick in the correct box to show which sentences are *true* and which are *false*.

The Romans allowed Prasutagus to rule his kingdom.	True ✓	False
Boudicca was whipped by the Romans.	True ✓	False
Boudicca's army was victorious in the Battle of Watling Street.	True ✓	False

MULTIPLE CHOICE

Circle the correct answer to the following question.

What was the Roman name for St Albans?

| Londoninium | (Verulamium) | Camulodunum | St Albans |

SEQUENCING

Look at *Boudicca*. Number the statements from 1 to 3 to show the order they occur in the text.

Although she lived almost 2,000 years ago, Boudicca will never be forgotten.	3
This warrior woman, who stood up to the might of the Roman army, is the perfect example of someone who never gave up and never surrendered.	1
A statue in remembrance of her was erected in Westminster, London, in 1902.	2

FIND AND COPY

Read the sentence below. Find and copy a word that suggests that the Romans were greatly outnumbered.

It seemed that the Romans didn't stand a chance: they were vastly outnumbered.

vastly

UNDERLINE OR HIGHLIGHT

Read the sentence below. Underline or highlight a word that means to receive something from someone who has died.

Only men could <u>inherit</u> land by Roman law, so they seized control of the whole kingdom.

ANSWERS

1. THE LAKE DISTRICT
FILL IN THE GAP
England
lakes
visitors
protected
Windermere
steep
rainfall
proudly
adventure
famous
canoeing
billion

MATCHING

Lake District	the Lakes
Lake Windermere	largest lake in England
Scafell Pike	England's highest mountain
Seathwaite	highest rate of rainfall

visitors per year	over 15 million
above sea level	978 m
largest lake	18 km
rate of rainfall	355 cm per year

William Wordsworth	I Wandered Lonely as a Cloud
Beatrix Potter	Peter Rabbit
orienteering	hiking race
gorge walking	scramble down into rivers

MULTIPLE CHOICE
over 15 million
pure
to enjoy the amazing sight
18 km
Beatrix Potter
Seathwaite
red squirrels
2017

TRUE OR FALSE
1. False
2. False
3. False
4. True
5. False
6. False
7. True
8. False
9. True
10. False
11. True
12. False
13. True
14. True
15. True

2. ANGLO-SAXONS
FILL IN THE GAP
invasions
customs
village
tribe
King
powerful
England
languages
tended
punished
read
crossed

MATCHING

new invaders arrived	410 CE
Vikings invaded Britain	787 to 1066
partially populated by warriors from Gaul	200 BCE to 43 CE
King Edward died	1066

Angles	southern Denmark
Saxons	Germany and the Netherlands
Vikings	Denmark and Norway
Jutes	northern Danes

girls	cooking meals
boys	same trade as fathers
adult	age of ten
Angle-land	England

MULTIPLE CHOICE
Europe
customs
Edward
ten
North Sea
Harald Hardrada
1066
the Vikings

TRUE OR FALSE
1. True
2. True
3. False
4. False
5. True
6. True
7. True
8. True
9. True
10. False
11. False
12. True
13. True
14. False
15. False

FIND AND COPY
settlers
arrived
tended
impact

UNDERLINE OR HIGHLIGHT
divided
kings
army
immediately
exhausted

3. RAMADAN AND EID

FILL IN THE GAP

religion
dawn
end
eat
Mosques
journey
Fasting
charity
ninth
lunar
difficulty
prayer

MATCHING

Muslim	follower of Islam
Islam	second-largest religion
Eid	huge celebration
Ramadan	ninth month

Islamic calendar	lunar calendar
difficulty of fasting helps	focus on their faith
not required to fast	very young or very old
fasting shows	devotion to faith

Mecca	holy city
fasting	between dawn and sunset
sweet foods	popular
lunar calendar	cycles of the moon

LABEL

Mecca
Eid
Five Pillars of Islam
Muslim
Islam
month
sweet foods
Eid
three days
ninth
Islam
dawn till sunset

SEQUENCING

3, 2, 1, 4
1, 2, 4, 3, 5
5, 1, 3, 4, 2

FIND AND COPY

population
vow
popular
celebration

UNDERLINE OR HIGHLIGHT

fast
difficulty
sunset
vary
faith

4. GUIDE DOGS

LABEL

6
1
4
3
5
2
Golden Retriever / Labrador / German Shepherd
1930
Dorothy Eustis
Muriel Crooke and Rosamund Bond
blind or partially-sighted people
14 months

SEQUENCING

2, 4, 1, 3
4, 1, 2, 5, 3
1, 3, 5, 2, 4

MULTIPLE CHOICE

1930
four
seven
being matched to an owner
St Bernard
distracted
14 months
44,600

TRUE OR FALSE

1. False
2. True
3. False
4. True
5. True
6. False
7. False
8. True
9. True
10. True
11. False
12. False
13. True
14. True
15. True

FIND AND COPY

companionship
protection
interact
partially-sighted

UNDERLINE OR HIGHLIGHT

dedicated
test
suitable
obedient
distracted

5. CHIMPANZEES
FILL IN THE GAP
comb
45
MATCHING
chimpanzee who went into space	Ham
used by chimpanzees to open nuts	rocks
chimpanzees feel	complex emotions

LABEL
700,000
1969
1961
45
20
TRUE OR FALSE
True
True
False
MULTIPLE CHOICE
four years
SEQUENCING
2, 1, 3
FIND AND COPY
taught
UNDERLINE OR HIGHLIGHT
comfortable

6. COUNTRY STUDY: RUSSIA
FILL IN THE GAP
oceans
tundra
MATCHING
fish eggs	caviar
mountain range	Altai
capital city	Moscow

LABEL
147 million
11
3,700 km
12.2 million
Yatutsk
TRUE OR FALSE
True
False
False
MULTIPLE CHOICE
caviar
SEQUENCING
2, 1, 3
FIND AND COPY
breathtakingly
UNDERLINE OR HIGHLIGHT
maritime

7. BOUDICCA
FILL IN THE GAP
Queen
Prasutagus
Rome
MATCHING
Londinium	London
Camulodunum	Colchester
Verulamium	St Albans

LABEL
Boudicca
Prasutagus
Anglesey
Boudicca
1902
TRUE OR FALSE
True
True
False
MULTIPLE CHOICE
Verulamium
SEQUENCING
1, 3, 2
FIND AND COPY
vastly
UNDERLINE OR HIGHLIGHT
inherit